PIANO • VOCAL • GUITAR

NEIL DIAMOND
Tennessee Moon

Cover photo by Jeff Dunas

ISBN 0-7935-6362-3

HAL•LEONARD™
CORPORATION
7777 W. BLUEMOUND RD. P.O. BOX 13819 MILWAUKEE, WI 53213

NEIL DIAMOND
Tennessee Moon

TENNESSEE MOON

Words and Music by NEIL DIAMOND
and DENNIS MORGAN

ONE GOOD LOVE

Words and Music by NEIL DIAMOND
and GARY NICHOLSON

It took a while ___ for me to
I fol-lowed all _____ life's pleas-

know
ures

what I was look-ing for. ___
wher-ev - er they would lead. ___

___ And ev - 'ry heart ___ I've ___
But some - one I ____ can ___

SHAME

Words and Music by NEIL DIAMOND
and HAL KETCHUM

hurt you with their lies, __ but words don't _ count at all.

'Cause I don't _ care _ what they say; there ain't _ no shame in lov-ing you. *Instrumental solo*

24

A MATTER OF LOVE

Words and Music by NEIL DIAMOND
and TOM SHAPIRO

MARRY ME

Words and Music by NEIL DIAMOND
and TOM SHAPIRO

DEEP INSIDE OF YOU

Words and Music by NEIL DIAMOND
and BETH NIELSEN CHAPMAN

GOLD DON'T RUST

Words and Music by NEIL DIAMOND,
GARY BURR and BOB DiPIERO

know you wor - ry ev - 'ry time __ I __ go _____ a - way.
wish that I __ could give __ you what __ you __ need _____ from me. __

LIKE YOU DO

Words and Music by SANDY KNOX
and STEVE ROSEN

Love nev-er doubts or suf-fers or cries. Love shows no fear, love
Love does-n't have un-ap-proach-a-ble walls or a heart that beck-ons and
Love nev-er threat-ens or fright-ens me. It's not held to-geth-er with a-

tells no lies. ___ And love would nev-er leave me in the dark. No,
then with-draws. ___ And love would nev-er steal my dig-ni-ty. Love has
pol-o-gies. ___ Love nev-er screams my name. No, and

love nev-er breaks my heart
nev-er made a fool of me like you
love nev-er turns a - way

do, like you do. do, like

you do. Oh, and I have _ known _ times when _

love seems un - sure. But when love is ___ un -
But where love may be un -

CAN ANYBODY HEAR ME

Words and Music by NEIL DIAMOND
and BILL LaBOUNTY

You got to take your time, now,
riv - er
Instrumental solo
if love is gon - na
and hear the riv - er

take you   by   the hand. __   You need to take your time, though,
call - in'   out   her name. __   I'm try - in' to for - give her,

WIN THE WORLD

Words and Music by NEIL DIAMOND
and SUSAN LONGACRE

I was al-ways try'n' to win the world, _ but

some-where I lost ____ you. ('Cause) I nev-er saw ____ you

on-ly try'n' to win my love. _____

It

NO LIMIT

Words and Music by NEIL DIAMOND
and RICHARD BENNETT

Some things got to be known. __
Me, I got to get out. __

REMINISCE FOR A WHILE

Words and Music by NEIL DIAMOND
and RAUL MALO

KENTUCKY WOMAN

Words and Music by
NEIL DIAMOND

Ken-tuck - y wom - an, she shines with her own
Well, she ain't the kind makes heads turn at the drop.

IF I LOST MY WAY

Words and Music by NEIL DIAMOND
and GARY BURR

EVERYBODY

Words and Music by NEIL DIAMOND
and JESSE DIAMOND

Ev - 'ry - bod - y needs some - one that they're gon - na be -
Ev - 'ry - bod - y needs some - one, but it's got - ta mean

lieve in.   Ev - 'ry - bod - y's the same a -
some - thing.   Giv - ing up a piece of you's the

'cause I would 've been no - where. Be - in' here all a - lone's a
that they're gon- na be - lieve in. Ev - 'ry-bod-y's the same a -

lone - ly sound.
round the world.

2nd time - rit.

TALKING OPTIMIST BLUES
(GOOD DAY TODAY)

Words and Music by NEIL DIAMOND
and GRETCHEN PETERS

(1.) *Instrumental solo-1st time*
(2.) Hey, I'm gon - na have a good day to - day.

Me, I'm gon - na have a good time

an - y - way. Put it all be -

hind me, lay it all a - way.

OPEN WIDE THESE PRISON DOORS

Words and Music by NEIL DIAMOND
and STEWART HARRIS

Moderately slow

Tied by love __ to you, __ but I was tied __ too strong. __
You were al - ways car-ing, al-ways warm __ and kind. __

Still, I'm a - fraid __ of know-in' what leav - in' means. __
But that was long __ a - go __ when love was blind. __

BLUE HIGHWAY

Words and Music by NEIL DIAMOND
and HARLAN HOWARD

So long, __ big cit-y; it's time to say __ good-bye. __
So long, __ con-fu-sion; it's time to slow __ things down. __

Instrumental solo

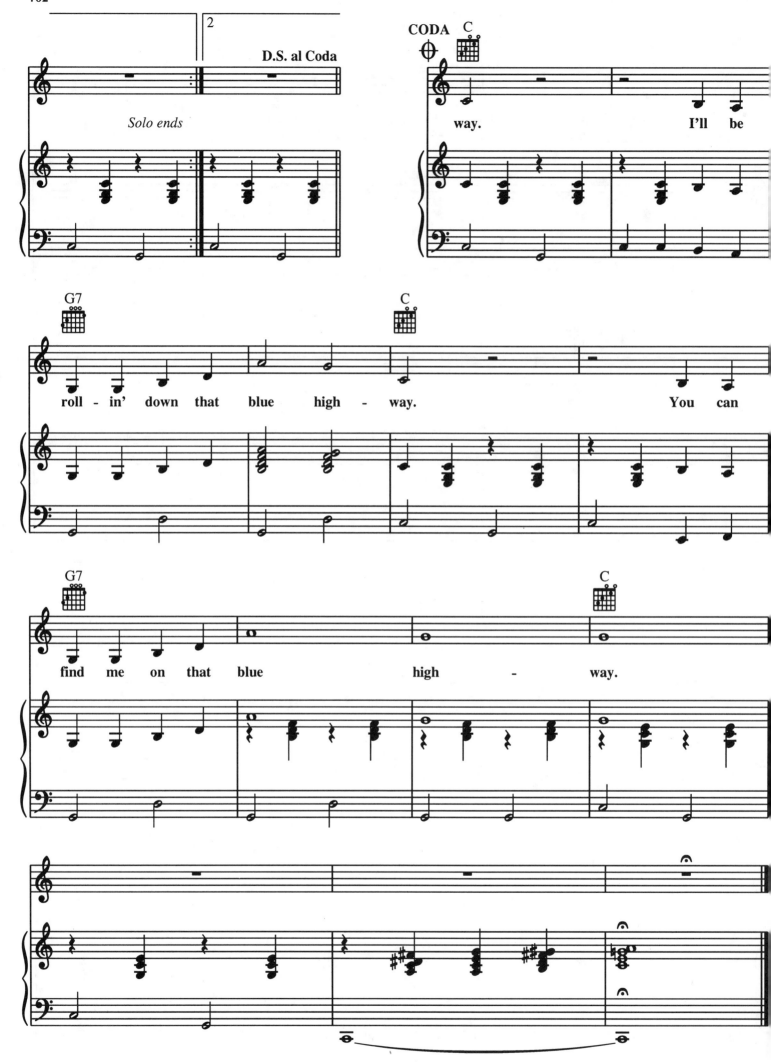